GRAPHIC NON[

JULIUS CAESAR

THE LIFE OF A ROMAN GENERAL

BOOK HOUSE

Designed and produced by
David West Children's Books,
7 Princeton Court,
55 Felsham Road,
London, SW15 1AZ

Editor: Gail Bushnell
Photo Research: Carlotta Cooper

Photo credits:
Pages 6 (both), 7, 44 (top) – Mary Evans Picture Library
Page 45 (bottom) – Rex Features Ltd.

First published in 2005 by **Book House**,
an imprint of **The Salariya Book Company Ltd**
25 Marlborough Place, Brighton BN1 1UB

Please visit the Salariya Book Company at:
www.salariya.com

HB ISBN 1 904642 81 0
PB ISBN 1 904642 82 9

Visit our website at **www.book-house.co.uk**
for free electronic versions of:
You wouldn't want to be an Egyptian Mummy!
You wouldn't want to be a Roman Gladiator!
Avoid joining Shackleton's Polar Expedition!

Due to the changing nature of internet links, the Salariya Book Company has developed an online list of websites related to the subject of this book. This site is updated regularly. Please use this link to access the list:
http://www.book-house.co.uk/gnf/caesar

A catalogue record for this book is available from the British Library.

Printed on paper from sustainable forests.

Manufactured in China.

CONTENTS

WHO'S WHO

Gaius Julius Caesar (100 BC-44 BC) Roman general and leader who conquered Gaul and defeated his fellow Romans in civil war. He was assassinated by Roman senators.

Pompey (106 BC-48 BC) Famous Roman general and onetime ally of Caesar. He became Caesar's enemy and main rival for power. He was murdered in Egypt.

Marcus Lucinius Crassus (105 BC-53 BC) Together with Caesar and Pompey, the rich Crassus formed a powerful triumvirate that ruled Rome.

Marcus Tullius Cicero (106 BC-43 BC) A writer, politician, and philosopher. Much of what we know about Caesar comes from Cicero's writings. He supported Pompey rather than Caesar and was later murdered.

Cleopatra (c. 70 BC-30 BC) Egyptian queen, friend, and companion of Caesar. They had a son, Caesarion. She later fell in love with Mark Antony.

Marcus Iunius Brutus (85 BC-42 BC) Leader of the conspirators against Caesar. He killed himself after being defeated by Mark Antony.

THE ROMAN WORLD – 44 BC

*T*he main map shows the Roman world at the time of Caesar's death in 44 BC. At this time, the Romans ruled most of the land around the Mediterranean Sea. For the next 300 years, they expanded the empire farther east and north, including Britain. Roman territory is shown in red.

POWER THROUGH CONQUEST

War was part of the Roman way of life. When the Romans had beaten an enemy, they made them part of the Roman state. Rome became very powerful this way. In time, they conquered the other great powers to become rulers of the Mediterranean and beyond.

ROMAN PROVINCES

The Latin word *provincia* used to mean responsibility. Roman officials based outside Rome were given the responsibility of collecting tributes, or taxes, from the people they governed. At first, cities that joined Rome shared its riches. As time went on, their lands were taken over and the people had no choice but to live like Romans.

THE CONQUEST OF GAUL

We know a lot about Caesar's conquest of Gaul because he wrote in great detail about the eight years he spent there. Caesar's greatest challenge came in 52 BC at the battle at Alesia. Gaul is modern-day France.

FURTHER SPAIN

Aduatuca •
THE EBURONES

Munda •

THE NERVII

THE BELGAE

ENGLISH CHANNEL

THE TREVIRI

THE PARISII

Seine R. • Duocortorum
THE SEQUANI

THE CARNUTES

Saone R.

THE VENETI

Alesia •

THE AEDUI

Bibracte •

Loire R.

THE HELVETII

QUIBERON BAY

Gergovia •

Rhone R.

PLAN OF ANCIENT ROME

The city of Rome included many hilltop villages. The most important one was on top of the Palatine Hill. It overlooked a crossing point on the River Tiber. Caesar's Rome had plumbing, paved streets, and grand buildings.

WALL OF SERVIUS TULLUS

Pompey's Theatre

Temple of Venus Genetrix

CAPITOLINE HILL

FORUM JULIUM

FORUM ROMANUM

PALATINE HILL

Caesar's house used by Cleopatra

RIVER TIBER

AVENTINE HILL

BRITAIN

Dover

Rhine R.

LUGDUNENSIS

GAUL

• Alesia

• Bibracte

Gergovia

TRANSALPINE GAUL

CISALPINE GAUL

Plancentia

Lucca •

Rubicon R.

ILLYRICUM

Rome • • Corfinium

ITALY

Dyrrhachium

MACEDONIA

BITHNYIA- PONTOS

• Thessalonica

• Pharsalus

EPIRUS

ASIA

CILICIA

SYRIA

AFRICA NOVA

AFRICA

• Carthage

• Thapsus

MEDITERRANEAN SEA

• Rhodes

CYPRUS

Alexandria •

Pelusium

EGYPT

PLAN OF ALEXANDRIA

Lighthouse of Alexandria
The Great Harbour
Pharos Island
Causeway (mole)
Royal palace

1
2
3
4
5

N
E
W
S

THE GREAT REPUBLIC

*T*he Romans overthrew their last Etruscan king in 509 BC and set up a republic so they could rule themselves. This democratic form of government was very important to the Romans.

THE ORIGINS OF ROME

Legend tells us that Rome was founded on seven hills by Romulus and Remus, twin brothers descended from the god Mars. Abandoned in the wild, they were raised by a wolf. Romulus killed Remus and became the first king of Rome in 753 BC. History, however, tells us that Rome was probably formed from two or more hill villages of the Latini tribe that were well placed on the River Tiber. Rome was then ruled by Etruscan kings for 100 years.

Romulus was one of the legendary founders of Rome.

ROMAN DEMOCRACY

When the Romans forced out the last Etruscan king, Tarquin the Proud, they became a republic – a state where the people choose their own rulers. The ruling Roman Senate consisted of 100 men from patrician, or noble, families. They gave power to two consuls, who served for a year only. They also elected judges, treasurers, and other officials. In Caesar's time, there were two main political groups in the Senate. They were called the *optimates* and the *populares*. The *optimates* were conservative. The *populares* used the backing of the People's Assembly to get things done.

A senator dressed in a toga practises the art of public speaking. It was a necessary skill for anyone hoping to rise up the political ladder.

THE POLITICAL LADDER

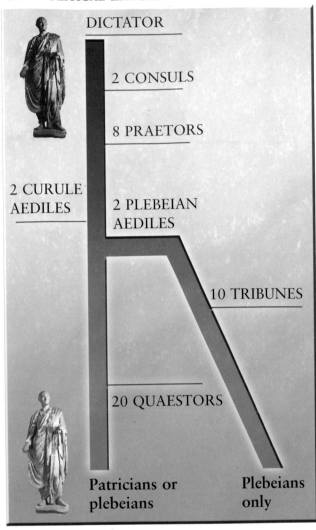

DICTATOR

2 CONSULS

8 PRAETORS

2 CURULE AEDILES

2 PLEBEIAN AEDILES

10 TRIBUNES

20 QUAESTORS

Patricians or plebeians

Plebeians only

*In Caesar's time, the Senate had 600 members. This chart shows the 45 serving officials in the Senate. The rest of the Senate was made up of people who had served in the past. A young man might start as a **quaestor**, a financial administrator often working outside Rome. Rising to an **aedile** (or **curule aedile** if his family was patrician), he could be in charge of public games or grain supplies. As a **praetor**, he served as a judge before becoming a **propraetor**, governing a small province. Afterward, he could run for election as a **consul**. At first, plebeians, or poorer citizens, had very little say in the republic. Later they were represented by the **tribunes**. **Consuls** were both judges and generals. They could elect a single **dictator** in times of emergency.*

A QUEST FOR POWER

Historians describe Julius Caesar in such different ways that it is hard to know just what sort of man he was. Born into a noble, patrician family, he claimed to be descended from the gods. Caesar was certainly ambitious, ruthless, and cruel. He was also highly intelligent and witty. He was tall and fair-haired with piercing brown eyes. His adoring troops were prepared to die for him.

This engraving of Caesar shows him with a laurel wreath on his head – the Roman symbol of victory. Caesar was an outstanding military leader.

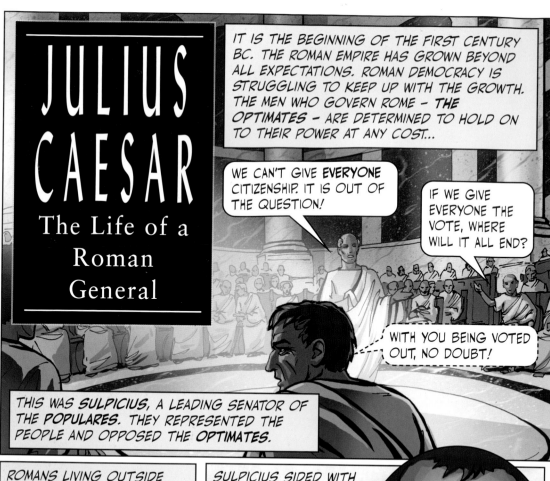

JULIUS CAESAR
The Life of a Roman General

IT IS THE BEGINNING OF THE FIRST CENTURY BC. THE ROMAN EMPIRE HAS GROWN BEYOND ALL EXPECTATIONS. ROMAN DEMOCRACY IS STRUGGLING TO KEEP UP WITH THE GROWTH. THE MEN WHO GOVERN ROME – **THE OPTIMATES** – ARE DETERMINED TO HOLD ON TO THEIR POWER AT ANY COST...

WE CAN'T GIVE **EVERYONE** CITIZENSHIP. IT IS OUT OF THE QUESTION!

IF WE GIVE EVERYONE THE VOTE, WHERE WILL IT ALL END?

WITH YOU BEING VOTED OUT, NO DOUBT!

THIS WAS **SULPICIUS**, A LEADING SENATOR OF THE **POPULARES**. THEY REPRESENTED THE PEOPLE AND OPPOSED THE **OPTIMATES**.

ROMANS LIVING OUTSIDE ROME DID NOT LIKE THE WAY THEY WERE RULED. IN 92 BC A **SOCIAL WAR** HAD BROKEN OUT. ROME PUT AN END TO IT, BUT IT HAPPENED AGAIN FOUR YEARS LATER WHEN SULPICIUS AND THE POPULARES TRIED TO FIGHT THEIR WAY INTO POWER.

SULPICIUS SIDED WITH THE MOST SUCCESSFUL GENERAL OF THE DAY – GAIUS MARIUS. AS A REWARD, SULPICIUS OFFERED HIM THE EASTERN COMMAND IN THE WAR AGAINST KING MITHRIDATES OF PONTUS.

HOWEVER, THE COMMAND HAD ALREADY BEEN OFFERED TO **LUCIUS SULLA**, THE TOP GENERAL ON THE OPTIMATE SIDE. HE WAS NORTH OF ROME WHEN HE HEARD OF MARIUS'S APPOINTMENT...

LET ME PUT THIS TO THE MEN...

SULPICIUS HAS DECIDED TO LET MARIUS CHEAT THIS GREAT ARMY OUT OF MITHRIDATES'S RICHES. ARE YOU WILLING TO ACCEPT THIS?

HOORAAAY!

NO! LET US MARCH ON ROME!

SULLA AND HIS ARMY MARCHED TOWARDS THE CENTRE OF ROME. A YOUNG NOBLEMAN WATCHED FROM HIS WINDOW...

MOTHER, WHERE HAS UNCLE MARIUS GONE?

HE HAS GONE INTO HIDING. NO ONE CAN DEFEAT SULLA.

BUT DON'T WORRY, JULIUS. OUR TIME WILL COME.

SULPICIUS WAS BEHEADED AND THE VICTORIOUS SULLA LEFT ROME TO FIGHT MITHRIDATES. ONCE HE WAS GONE, MARIUS CAME OUT OF HIDING TO TAKE HIS PLACE. HE WAS SUPPORTED BY SENATOR CINNA.

MARIUS WAS AN OLD MAN NOW. WHEN HE DIED IN 87 BC, HE PASSED HIS POWER TO CINNA. CINNA GAVE HIS DAUGHTER, CORNELIA, IN MARRIAGE TO MARIUS'S NEPHEW, 16-YEAR-OLD JULIUS CAESAR.

CINNA GATHERED AN ARMY TO FIGHT SULLA ABROAD. BUT HE WAS KILLED SOON AFTER. IN 82 BC, SULLA RETURNED AND FOUGHT HIS WAY TO ROME. THEN HE MADE HIMSELF DICTATOR AND LOOKED TO PUNISH THE FOLLOWERS OF CINNA AND MARIUS.

SULLA SENT FOR CAESAR...

YOU SEEM TO HAVE DONE NOTHING AGAINST ME AND YOU SHOW GREAT PROMISE. I WILL HELP YOU FURTHER YOUR CAREER ON ONE CONDITION...

...THAT YOU DIVORCE CINNA'S DAUGHTER AND MARRY SOMEONE OF **MY** CHOOSING.

OTHERWISE...

I WILL **NOT**!

SO BE IT!

LATER...

SULLA, WHAT'S TO BE DONE ABOUT CAESAR?

DOES HE **STILL** REFUSE TO COOPERATE?

YES.

THAT BOY IS EVEN MORE OF A THREAT THAN HIS UNCLE MARIUS. HE **MUST DIE.**

LATER, AT CAESAR'S HOUSE...

SULLA MAY BE DICTATOR BUT HE IS NO CHILD-KILLER...

AURELIA, WE WILL WORK ON GETTING YOUR SON A PARDON...

...BUT HE MUST **LEAVE ROME.**

CAESAR'S FRIENDS WON HIM A PARDON. HE WENT TO FIGHT IN ASIA WHERE HE SHOWED HIMSELF TO BE AN EXCELLENT SOLDIER. HE ALSO MADE HIMSELF USEFUL BY SECURING SHIPS FROM THE KING OF BITHNIA. THEN IN 78 BC, CAME NEWS OF **SULLA'S DEATH.**

CAESAR, WHERE ARE YOU GOING?

HOME! IT'S TIME FOR ME TO MAKE A NAME FOR MYSELF!

ROME, THE FORUM – 78 BC.

...AND FURTHERMORE, IT IS CLEAR TO ME THAT THIS IS A CRIME OF THE...

WHY ARE WE WATCHING THIS, CICERO? YOU KNOW YOUNG CAESAR WILL LOSE HIS CASE.

PERHAPS! BUT LISTEN, HE SPEAKS SO WELL! MARK ME, HE WILL BE ONE TO WATCH.

CAESAR LOST HIS CASE, BUT HE PERFORMED WELL. HE DECIDED TO LEARN MORE ABOUT PUBLIC SPEAKING. HE WENT TO RHODES TO STUDY.

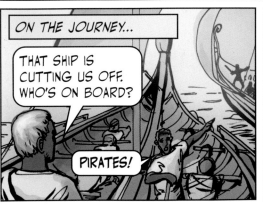

ON THE JOURNEY...

THAT SHIP IS CUTTING US OFF. WHO'S ON BOARD?

PIRATES!

THE PIRATES WERE VERY PLEASED TO CAPTURE A YOUNG NOBLEMAN. THEY PROMPTLY HELD CAESAR FOR RANSOM...

HOW MUCH DO THEY WANT FOR ME?

20 TALENTS.

HA! I'M WORTH MORE THAN THAT!

TELL THEM TO ASK FOR 50! AND THAT I'LL BE BACK TO STRING THEM ALL UP AS SOON AS I'M FREED.

ONCE FREED, CAESAR GATHERED SOME SOLDIERS AND RETURNED TO THE PIRATES' DEN. HE TOOK THE PIRATES' MONEY AND HAD THEM CRUCIFIED. SHOWING MERCY BECAUSE THEY HAD TREATED HIM WELL, CAESAR HAD THEIR THROATS CUT FIRST.

IN 71 BC, CAESAR'S AUNT JULIA AND HIS WIFE, CORNELIA, DIED WITHIN A SHORT TIME OF EACH OTHER. THEIR DEATHS LEFT HIM WITH A YOUNG DAUGHTER TO RAISE. CAESAR SPOKE AT BOTH FUNERALS, EVEN THOUGH THE JOB USUALLY WENT TO A WOMAN. HE USED THE OPPORTUNITY TO ATTACK THE RULING CLASS.

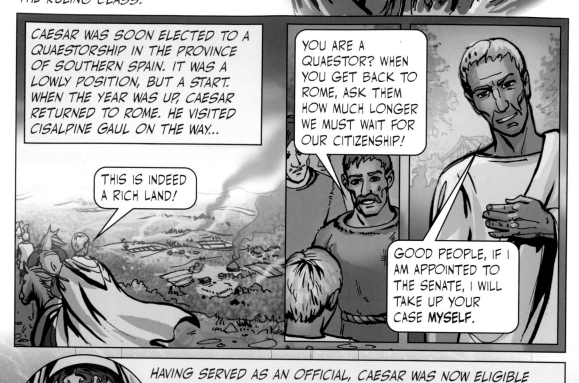

CAESAR WAS SOON ELECTED TO A QUAESTORSHIP IN THE PROVINCE OF SOUTHERN SPAIN. IT WAS A LOWLY POSITION, BUT A START. WHEN THE YEAR WAS UP, CAESAR RETURNED TO ROME. HE VISITED CISALPINE GAUL ON THE WAY...

THIS IS INDEED A RICH LAND!

YOU ARE A QUAESTOR? WHEN YOU GET BACK TO ROME, ASK THEM HOW MUCH LONGER WE MUST WAIT FOR OUR CITIZENSHIP!

GOOD PEOPLE, IF I AM APPOINTED TO THE SENATE, I WILL TAKE UP YOUR CASE **MYSELF**.

HAVING SERVED AS AN OFFICIAL, CAESAR WAS NOW ELIGIBLE FOR LIFELONG MEMBERSHIP TO THE SENATE, THE 600-STRONG GOVERNING BODY OF THE EMPIRE. CAESAR WAS APPOINTED, BUT HE ALSO WANTED TO HAVE **INFLUENCE**. FOR THIS HE NEEDED **MONEY**. IN 67 BC, HE MARRIED **POMPEIA**, THE RICH GRANDDAUGHTER OF SULLA. NOW ALL HE NEEDED WERE THE RIGHT **POLITICAL FRIENDS**.

SOON, CAESAR SAW HIS CHANCE. POMPEY, THE POWERFUL EX-CONSUL, WAS IN LINE FOR A JOB. AT A SENATE MEETING...

THE PIRATES OF THE MEDITERRANEAN ARE RUINING OUR COMMUNICATIONS. KING MITHRIDATES IS BEHIND THEM...

...I SUGGEST THAT WE GIVE **POMPEY** A NAVY TO GET RID OF THEM ONCE AND FOR ALL!

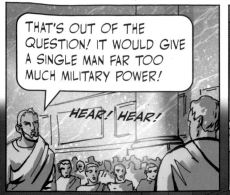

THAT'S OUT OF THE QUESTION! IT WOULD GIVE A SINGLE MAN FAR TOO MUCH MILITARY POWER!

HEAR! HEAR!

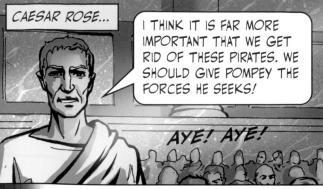

CAESAR ROSE...

I THINK IT IS FAR MORE IMPORTANT THAT WE GET RID OF THESE PIRATES. WE SHOULD GIVE POMPEY THE FORCES HE SEEKS!

AYE! AYE!

AND SO IT WAS. POMPEY WAS VERY SUCCESSFUL. THREE MONTHS LATER, HE CAME BACK WITH AN IDEA...

...AND NOW LET ME GO AFTER THE REAL POWER BEHIND THESE PIRATES – KING MITHRIDATES HIMSELF!

THIS TIME, CICERO ROSE...

MITHRIDATES HAS LONG BEEN A THORN IN OUR SIDE. I HAVE NO PROBLEM WITH AGREEING TO ANY ACTION THAT WOULD STOP HIM AND PROVIDE US WITH HIS RICHES!

THE SENATE AGREED.

WHILE POMPEY WAS AWAY, CAESAR MADE FRIENDS WITH POMPEY'S ENEMY IN THE SENATE – THE RICH BUSINESSMAN, CRASSUS.

CRASSUS HELPED CAESAR BECOME CURULE AEDILE AND LENT HIM THE MONEY TO STAGE IMPRESSIVE PUBLIC GAMES. THESE SHOWS MADE CAESAR VERY POPULAR.

WONDERFUL SHOW, CAESAR!

URRGH!

HOORAY FOR CAESAR!

USING MORE OF CRASSUS'S MONEY, CAESAR BECAME CHIEF PRIEST. NOW HE HAD A REAL CHANCE OF POWER.

CAESAR MOVED INTO THE CHIEF PRIEST'S OFFICIAL HOUSE.

AT LAST, IT BEGINS!

LATER IN 62 BC, CAESAR WAS ELECTED TO THE OFFICE OF PRAETOR. CRASSUS WAS PLEASED...

WELL DONE! YOU'RE ONLY ONE STEP AWAY FROM CONSUL NOW!

TO BE ELECTED A CONSUL, AND BE AT THE HEAD OF THE SENATE, WAS CAESAR'S GOAL.

MEANWHILE, SEVERAL WOMEN WERE AT THE CAESAR HOUSEHOLD FOR A SACRED CELEBRATION...

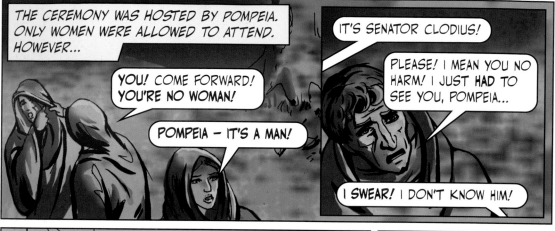

THE CEREMONY WAS HOSTED BY POMPEIA. ONLY WOMEN WERE ALLOWED TO ATTEND. HOWEVER...

YOU! COME FORWARD! YOU'RE NO WOMAN!

POMPEIA – IT'S A MAN!

IT'S SENATOR CLODIUS!

PLEASE! I MEAN YOU NO HARM! I JUST HAD TO SEE YOU, POMPEIA...

I SWEAR! I DON'T KNOW HIM!

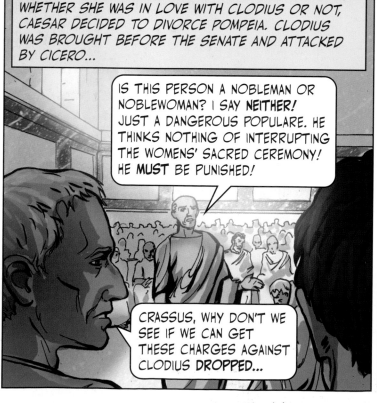

WHETHER SHE WAS IN LOVE WITH CLODIUS OR NOT, CAESAR DECIDED TO DIVORCE POMPEIA. CLODIUS WAS BROUGHT BEFORE THE SENATE AND ATTACKED BY CICERO...

IS THIS PERSON A NOBLEMAN OR NOBLEWOMAN? I SAY NEITHER! JUST A DANGEROUS POPULARE. HE THINKS NOTHING OF INTERRUPTING THE WOMENS' SACRED CEREMONY! HE MUST BE PUNISHED!

CRASSUS, WHY DON'T WE SEE IF WE CAN GET THESE CHARGES AGAINST CLODIUS DROPPED...

WHY?

HE WOULD BE VERY GRATEFUL. THAT COULD BE VERY USEFUL TO US.

CAESAR COULDN'T RESIST SCHEMING. NOW CLODIUS OWED HIM A BIG FAVOUR.

CAESAR HAD SERVED AS A PRAETOR. PRAETORS, LIKE THE CONSULS ABOVE THEM, WERE REWARDED WITH THE RIGHT TO GOVERN A PROVINCE FOR ONE YEAR. IN 61 BC, CAESAR LEFT TO GOVERN SOUTHERN SPAIN. HE HOPED TO MAKE ENOUGH MONEY FIGHTING THE SPANISH TRIBES TO PAY OFF HIS DEBTS AND STAY CLOSE TO THE IMPORTANT SENATORS IN ROME WHO COULD HELP HIM BECOME CONSUL.

HIS PLAN PAID OFF. IN 60 BC, CAESAR RETURNED TO ROME. HE WAS CONFIDENT THAT HE WOULD BE ELECTED AS ONE OF THE TWO CONSULS FOR 59 BC.

HIS ENEMIES IN THE SENATE WERE READY FOR HIM. THEY MADE SURE THAT THE CONSULS FOR 59 BC WOULD GOVERN ONLY WORTHLESS AREAS OF FORESTLAND INSTEAD OF RICH PROVINCES.

THE FORMER CONSUL, POMPEY WAS SNUBBED TOO. THE SENATE REFUSED TO GIVE HIS SOLDIERS THE LAND OWED TO THEM AS A REWARD FOR THEIR SERVICE.

CRASSUS WAS ALSO TURNED DOWN WHEN HE ASKED FOR LOWER TAXES FOR HIS KNIGHTS' FARMERS.

CAESAR'S NEXT STEP WAS TO BRING TOGETHER POMPEY AND CRASSUS. THEY HAD BEEN ENEMIES, BUT CAESAR USED THEIR SHARED ANGER AT THE SENATE TO CONVINCE THEM TO FORM A TRIUMVIRATE.

CICERO REFUSED.

SO WHY AREN'T YOU JOINING THEM, CICERO?

I CAN'T! POMPEY IS TOO FULL OF HIMSELF...

...AND CRASSUS HAS ONLY HIS OWN INTERESTS AT HEART. AS FOR CAESAR, HE'S ONE TO FEAR...

...AS ONE FEARS THE SMILING SURFACE OF THE DEADLY SEA.

THEN CAESAR ASKED CICERO TO JOIN THEM...

ONCE CAESAR HAD BEEN MADE CONSUL, HE PUT ON HIS NEW TOGA...

...CROSSED FROM THE VIA SACRA TO THE CAPITOL...

...AND SAT IN THE SENATE'S OFFICIAL CONSULAR CHAIR.

NEXT TO CAESAR WAS THE OTHER CONSUL, HIS OUTSPOKEN ENEMY, **BIBULUS.** CAESAR ROSE TO PROPOSE HIS FIRST LAW...

I WANT TO CREATE A COMMISSION...

...TO BUY LAND FOR RETIRED SOLDIERS. THIS IS AN OLD IDEA FOR A LAW, PUT FORWARD BY **SULLA HIMSELF.**

IT WILL BE PAID FOR PARTLY WITH MONEY FROM POMPEY'S SPOILS. SO, **UNLIKE** SULLA'S, MY LAW WILL ROB NO ONE!

AS SOON AS CAESAR SAT DOWN, **CATO,** A RESPECTED SENATOR, GOT UP TO SPEAK...

I SAY, LET THINGS BE DONE AS THEY HAVE ALWAYS BEEN, AND FURTHERMORE...

CATO SPOKE ON AND ON UNTIL THE SUN WAS NEARLY DOWN.

HE WAS TRYING TO STOP THE LAW FROM BEING PASSED.

CAESAR SNAPPED...

ARREST THAT MAN!

CATO WAS RELEASED AND THE LAW WAS PUT TO A VOTE. DURING THE VOTING, BIBULUS TRIED TO INTERFERE, BUT HE WAS HURLED DOWN THE STEPS AND SMELLY HORSE DUNG WAS THROWN AT HIM.

CAESAR'S LAW WAS PASSED.

AND SO THE PATTERN WAS SET FOR CAESAR'S YEAR AS CONSUL. WHETHER IT WAS HIS STRONG WILL IN THE SENATE OR GANG LAW ON THE STREETS, CAESAR DID EVERYTHING TO GET HIS CHANGES THROUGH. HE MARRIED **CALPURNIA**, THE DAUGHTER OF THE NEXT CONSUL, PISO. HE ALSO OFFERED HIS DAUGHTER, JULIA, AS A WIFE TO POMPEY. ALL THIS WOULD HELP HIM TO STAY POWERFUL IN THE FUTURE.

CAESAR STILL HAD THE PROBLEM OF NEXT YEAR'S GOVERNORSHIP. GOVERNING WORTHLESS FORESTS WAS JUST NOT PART OF HIS PLAN...

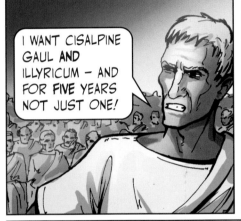

I WANT CISALPINE GAUL **AND** ILLYRICUM – AND FOR **FIVE** YEARS NOT JUST ONE!

CAESAR WENT OVER THE HEADS OF THE SENATE AND APPEALED TO THE PEOPLE. HE GOT WHAT HE WANTED – AND MORE...

...TRANSALPINE GAUL. THE THREE PROVINCES TOGETHER WOULD GIVE CAESAR AND HIS ARMY THE CHANCE TO WIN BATTLES THAT WOULD MAKE THEM RICH AND POWERFUL.

MEANWHILE, CAESAR HAD HIS EYE ON EGYPT.

KING PTOLEMY XII'S RULE WAS CRUMBLING. CAESAR OFFERED THE SUPPORT OF ROME AT A VERY HIGH PRICE. PTOLEMY ACCEPTED IT.

CAESAR'S WAYS WERE ALWAYS EXTREME. IF HE EVER BECAME A PRIVATE CITIZEN AGAIN, HE COULD BE TRIED FOR TREASON – AND **RUINED**.

AT THE END OF CAESAR'S CONSULSHIP, THE SENATE HELD AN INQUIRY INTO THE LAWS HE HAD PASSED. THEY COULDN'T AGREE ON ANYTHING.

THREE DAYS LATER...

I HAVE HAD **ENOUGH** OF WAITING FOR THESE FOOLS TO DECIDE WHAT TO DO. IT IS TIME TO GO!

CAESAR MARCHED HIS ARMY OUT OF ROME AND SET UP CAMP BEYOND CITY LIMITS. THIS MEANT HE WAS NOW A **PROCONSUL** AND FREE FROM ANY ACTION THAT THE SENATE TOOK AGAINST HIM. THREE MONTHS LATER, HE LEFT FOR GAUL.

THERE WAS NO TIME TO CELEBRATE. THE FIGHTING IN GAUL HAD ONLY JUST BEGUN...

LEADERS OF THE GAULS SAY THE GERMAN PRINCE, **ARIOVISTUS**, IS A THREAT.

THEN HE IS A THREAT TO THE ROMANS. WE MUST TALK TO THE GERMANS.

ONLY A YEAR EARLIER, CAESAR HAD WELCOMED ARIOVISTUS AS A FRIEND AND AN ALLY. NOW, CAESAR CALLED FOR A MEETING BUT ARIOVISTUS WAS TOO PROUD. HE ASKED CAESAR WHAT THE ROMANS WERE DOING IN "HIS" GAUL, AND HE REFUSED TO TALK.

CAESAR MARCHED HIS ARMY TO THE EDGE OF THE GERMAN CAMP...

WE WILL TRY TO DRAW THEM OUT.

A SHORT WHILE LATER...

THEY ARE COMING OUT TO FIGHT!

EXCELLENT! READY THE MEN.

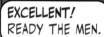

BUT THE GERMANS CAME OUT AT A RUN. IT WAS TOO LATE TO THROW JAVELINS...

WURRRAAAAGH!

THE GERMANS' DEFENCE WAS STRONG...

SHCLUNG!   KNNGG!

...BUT CAESAR'S MEN FOUGHT FIERCELY...

RIP!

AAAAGH!

THWACK!

...AND THE GERMANS WERE FORCED BACK ACROSS THE RHINE.

A FEW MONTHS LATER, AT CAESAR'S WINTER CAMP IN THE HEART OF GAUL...

TWO GREAT VICTORIES IN A SINGLE SEASON AND DOES THE SENATE APPRECIATE ME? NO!

SIR, WE HAVE WORD THAT THE BELGAE ARE MASSING A FORCE OF 300,000 AGAINST US!

MARVELLOUS!

THIS WAS A REAL CHANCE.

NOW CAESAR HAD A REASON TO TAKE ALL OF GAUL. WITH THE HELP OF TWO EXTRA LEGIONS, HE SET OUT TO FIGHT THE HUGE ARMY FORMED BY THE REBELLIOUS TRIBES.

ON ARRIVAL, HE FOUND THAT THE LARGE BELGAE ARMY HAD BROKEN UP. HIS MEN DEALT WITH THE SMALLER UNITS OF TRIBESMEN EASILY. BUT THE NERVII, THE BEST FIGHTERS, WERE NOWHERE TO BE SEEN.

CAESAR'S LEGIONS WERE PREPARING TO MAKE CAMP WHEN THE NERVII STRUCK...

WYRRRRAGHHH!

FLENCH!

THERE WASN'T TIME TO PUT ON ARMOUR.

CAESAR STRUGGLED TO COMMAND...

CENTURION, I CAN'T SEE! WHAT'S HAPPENING?

SIR, OUR RIGHT FLANK IS COLLAPSING. THE TRIBESMEN ARE BREAKING THROUGH!

GIVE ME THAT!

SNATCH!

NEWS OF CAESAR'S SUCCESS IN GAUL REACHED ROME. CLODIUS SPOKE IN THE SENATE...

CAESAR'S VICTORIES ARE EVEN **GREATER** THAN POMPEY'S!

I PROPOSE A FEAST IN CAESAR'S HONOUR. IT WILL LAST FOR 15 DAYS!

POMPEY HAD ONLY BEEN HONOURED WITH **10 DAYS** FOR HIS VICTORIES. CAESAR WANTED TO PREVENT JEALOUSY AND TO STRENGTHEN TIES WITH POMPEY AND CRASSUS. HE INVITED THEM TO A MEETING IN THE TOWN OF LUCCA.

POMPEY SPOKE FIRST...

THINGS ARE GOING WELL IN ROME. CLODIUS CONTROLS THE MOB, WHILE I HAVE THE SENATE FIRMLY IN MY GRIP!

HA! BUT FOR HOW MUCH LONGER, POMPEY? CICERO AND THE OTHERS ARE DETERMINED TO UNDO CAESAR'S LAWS.

THAT WILL NOT HAPPEN...

...IF BOTH OF YOU BECOME CONSULS AGAIN. THE THREE OF US MUST CONTINUE TO ACT TOGETHER.

CRASSUS, **YOU** SHOULD GOVERN THE PROVINCE OF SYRIA. YOU CAN START WAGING WAR AGAINST THE PARTHIANS.

POMPEY, **YOU** SHOULD HAVE THE TWO SPANISH PROVINCES. YOU CAN STAY IN ROME AND GOVERN THEM FROM THERE.

AND **YOU** CAESAR?

I NEED YOU TO HELP ME TO BECOME CONSUL AGAIN, WHILE I AM STILL GOVERNOR. IN THE MEANTIME, I JUST HAVE ONE LITTLE PROBLEM TO TAKE CARE OF...

THE VENETI TRIBE ON THE NORTH COAST OF GAUL WAS IN REVOLT. THEY DID GOOD TRADE WITH THE ISLAND OF BRITAIN, AND THEY WANTED TO PROTECT IT.

THE VENETI HAD A STRONG NAVY. CAESAR ORDERED LOCAL MEN ON THE RIVER LOIRE TO BUILD SHIPS AND TO HIRE OARSMEN AND STEERSMEN.

HOWEVER, CAESAR'S SPIES GAVE HIM WORRYING NEWS ABOUT THE ENEMY SHIPS...

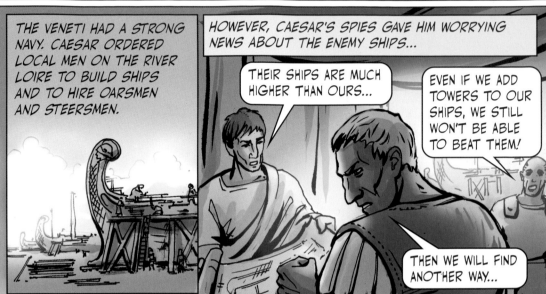

THEIR SHIPS ARE MUCH HIGHER THAN OURS...

EVEN IF WE ADD TOWERS TO OUR SHIPS, WE STILL WON'T BE ABLE TO BEAT THEM!

THEN WE WILL FIND ANOTHER WAY...

CAESAR WATCHED AS HIS NAVY FOUGHT THE VENETI...

...AND UNFOLDED ITS PLAN...

TAKE US RIGHT UP CLOSE. GRAPPLERS, WAIT FOR MY SIGNAL!

AS THEY PULLED ALONGSIDE...

SNAG!

NOW ROW AWAY HARD!

SNAP!

SNAP!

WITH ITS SAILS RIPPED DOWN, THE VENETI SHIP COULD NOT MOVE. THE ROMANS CLIMBED ON BOARD AND TOOK CONTROL. EACH VENETI SHIP WAS DESTROYED THIS WAY. IT WAS YET ANOTHER GREAT VICTORY FOR CAESAR IN GAUL.

A FEW MONTHS LATER, CAESAR CALLED HIS COMMANDERS TOGETHER...

HAS ANY ROMAN ACTUALLY BEEN TO THIS ISLAND OF **BRITAIN**?

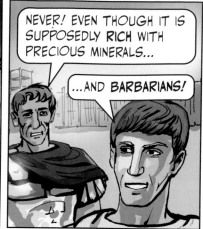

NEVER! EVEN THOUGH IT IS SUPPOSEDLY **RICH** WITH PRECIOUS MINERALS...

...AND **BARBARIANS**!

THEN WE WILL GO!

CAESAR'S FIRST ATTACK IN 55 BC WAS SPOILED BY A STORM. THE NEXT JULY, HE LANDED 800 SHIPS NEAR DOVER...

WHILE CAESAR MARCHED 80 MILES INLAND, THE STORMS CAME AGAIN.

HE DECIDED NOT TO RISK STAYING THE WINTER.

AM I TO BE DEFEATED...BY THE **WEATHER**?

CAESAR WAS ALSO BEATEN BACK BY THE BRITISH TRIBES. ONCE AGAIN, CAESAR FAILED TO CONQUER BRITAIN.

CAESAR'S TROOPS RETURNED TO GAUL AND SET UP SMALL CAMPS FOR THE WINTER.

SHORTLY, CAESAR RECEIVED NEWS FROM GAUL. THE EBURONE TRIBE HAD RISEN UP AND WIPED OUT A WHOLE ROMAN CAMP?

WITH OTHER TRIBES, THEY ATTACKED MORE CAMPS. LATE THE FOLLOWING YEAR, CAESAR MET WITH THE TRIBAL LEADERS...

ACCO OF THE SENONES...

I HEAR YOU HAVE JOINED THE EBURONES – SLAYERS OF MY MEN. I HEREBY SERVE NOTICE, THIS REBELLION IS OVER!

KILL HIM...

AAAAAAGGGGHHH!

YET THE REBELLION CONTINUED. IN 52 BC, CAESAR FACED HIS BIGGEST CHALLENGE IN GAUL...

VERCINGETORIX!

VERCINGETORIX WAS THE YOUNG KING OF GAUL. HE HAD AN ARMY OF MORE THAN 200,000 MEN. THEY DEFEATED CAESAR AT GERGOVIA AND BURNED HIS SUPPLIES. CAESAR SEEMED TO BE LOSING GAUL. THEN VERCINGETORIX WAS BEATEN BY CAESAR'S SOLDIERS. HE RETREATED TO THE HILL TOWN OF ALESIA...

LOOK AT IT, CAESAR. IT'S A NATURAL FORT. IT WILL BE IMPOSSIBLE TO TAKE!

THEN WE SHALL DIG!

THIRTY DAYS LATER, A LARGE ARMY OF GAULS ARRIVED TO SAVE ALESIA. HOWEVER, THEY FOUND THAT THE ROMAN ARMY HAD MANAGED TO BUILD DEFENCES AROUND IT.

THE ROMANS WERE OUTNUMBERED FOUR TO ONE. YET THEIR STRONG DEFENCES PROTECTED THEM FROM THE ATTACKS THAT WERE COMING FROM BOTH SIDES...FOR A WHILE.

THE GAULS FINALLY FOUND A WEAK SPOT. THEY SENT IN OVER 60,000 MEN AT THIS SPOT.

THE ROMANS BEGAN TO BUCKLE. THEN SUDDENLY, CAESAR HIMSELF APPEARED WITH A LEGION...

STAND FIRM! MEN! EVERYTHING WE'VE FOUGHT FOR IN GAUL DEPENDS UPON THIS DAY!

THE ROMANS FOUGHT HARD AND WON THE BATTLE. THE GAULS FLED. VERCINGETORIX SURRENDERED AND WAS PUT IN CHAINS. AFTER THE WAR, CAESAR WANTED GAUL TO BE PEACEFUL. MEANWHILE, BACK HOME, MUCH HAD HAPPENED.

CAESAR'S DAUGHTER, JULIA, HAD DIED. HE NO LONGER HAD A STRONG CONNECTION TO HER HUSBAND, POMPEY. CLODIUS HAD BEEN KILLED AND THE SENATE HOUSE SET ON FIRE. CRASSUS WAS KILLED BY THE PARTHIANS. CAESAR NEEDED NEW ALLIES.

HE FOUND ONE IN A TRIBUNE CALLED CURIO...

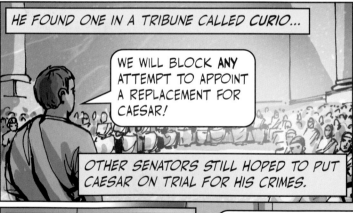

WE WILL BLOCK **ANY** ATTEMPT TO APPOINT A REPLACEMENT FOR CAESAR!

OTHER SENATORS STILL HOPED TO PUT CAESAR ON TRIAL FOR HIS CRIMES.

MEANWHILE, POMPEY HAD GONE BACK ON HIS PROMISE MADE AT LUCCA TO HELP CAESAR RUN FOR CONSUL WHILE STILL A GOVERNOR. IT WAS THE ONLY WAY CAESAR COULD RETURN TO POWER AND AVOID TRIAL.

CICERO WATCHED THESE EVENTS WITH CONCERN...

...WHILE CAESAR KNOWS THAT HIS **FUTURE** DEPENDS UPON KEEPING THEM BOTH.

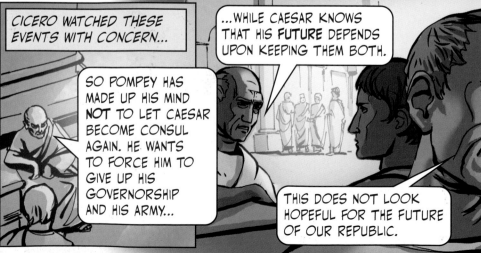

SO POMPEY HAS MADE UP HIS MIND **NOT** TO LET CAESAR BECOME CONSUL AGAIN. HE WANTS TO FORCE HIM TO GIVE UP HIS GOVERNORSHIP AND HIS ARMY...

THIS DOES NOT LOOK HOPEFUL FOR THE FUTURE OF OUR REPUBLIC.

IN 50 BC, CURIO FOUND SUPPORT FROM A NEW TRIBUNE CALLED **MARK ANTONY**. ANTONY SPOKE TO THE SENATE...

...THAT **BOTH** CAESAR **AND** POMPEY STAND DOWN AS GOVERNORS...

THE SENATE REFUSED.

THEN CONSUL **GAIUS MARCELLUS** STOOD UP...

IN THE INTEREST OF NATIONAL SECURITY, GOVERNOR POMPEY SHOULD BE GIVEN COMMAND OF OUR ARMY. AND WE SHOULD DEMAND THAT GOVERNOR CAESAR LAY DOWN HIS COMMAND...

THE SENATE AGREED.

POMPEY REPLIED.

...I ACCEPT THE COMMAND.

IN RESPONSE, CAESAR MOVED **HIS** ARMY CLOSER TO THE ITALIAN BORDER. HE SENT MARK ANTONY TO THE SENATE WITH A NEW MESSAGE...

BOOO! BOOO! BOOO!

PLEASE! WILL YOU **LET** ME SPEAK?

HE WAS SHOUTED DOWN.

THEN CAESAR WAS DECLARED A PUBLIC ENEMY. ALL OFFICIALS WERE CALLED TO THE DEFENCE OF ROME.

CURIO, THEY MEAN TO FORCE US TO COOPERATE!

THEN THERE'S ONLY ONE THING WE CAN DO...

...WE MUST GO TO CAESAR!

CAESAR WAS AT THE ITALIAN BORDER WITH AN ARMY AT HIS COMMAND.

THEY HALTED AT A RIVER CALLED THE RUBICON...

MEN! EVEN NOW WE MAY TURN BACK...

...BUT ONCE WE CROSS THIS BRIDGE...

...THE ISSUE IS WITH THE **SWORD!**

THEN CAESAR AND HIS ARMY **CROSSED THE RUBICON.** IT WAS AGAINST THE LAW OF ROME FOR A GOVERNOR TO MARCH HIS TROOPS ON THE MOTHER COUNTRY. IT COULD MEAN ONLY ONE THING – **CIVIL WAR.**

CHEER!
HOORAAY!
HAIL CAESAR!

...WHILE HIS ENEMIES LEFT ROME.

THE TWO CONSULS FLED TO MACEDONIA. POMPEY WENT SOUTH.

IN TOWN AFTER TOWN, THE PEOPLE OPENED THEIR ARMS TO CAESAR...

THE PEOPLE OF CORFINIUM TRIED TO FIGHT CAESAR WITHOUT SUCCESS. THE CAPTIVES KNELT BEFORE HIM.

I HAVE DECIDED THAT...

...YOU WILL BE SPARED.

I DO NOT WANT TO BE CRUEL LIKE SULLA! AND I DO NOT WANT TO BE HATED, AS HE WAS.

A FEW WEEKS LATER, POMPEY TOOK TWO LEGIONS AND JOINED HIS CONSULS IN MACEDONIA. IN ROME, CAESAR MET WITH CICERO...

YOUR TONGUE IS WORTH A LEGION. WILL YOU HELP ME?

THE MERCY YOU SHOWED AT CORFINIUM WAS IMPRESSIVE, BUT I CANNOT BE AGAINST THE REPUBLIC...

CAESAR WENT AWAY.

HE WANTS NOTHING LESS THAN TO BE KING OF ROME!

CAESAR CALLED A SPECIAL MEETING OF THE SENATE. NOT MANY SENATORS ATTENDED.

IF YOU WILL NOT HELP ME RUN THE COUNTRY...

I WILL RUN IT MYSELF!

THEN POMPEY ASKED FOR ALL SENATORS TO JOIN HIM IN THE SOUTH. MANY OLDER POLITICIANS, INCLUDING CICERO, WENT.

THEN...

CAESAR, OUR TROOPS ARE REBELLING AT PLACENTIA!

SADDLE MY HORSE!

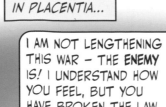

IN PLACENTIA...

I AM NOT LENGTHENING THIS WAR – THE ENEMY IS! I UNDERSTAND HOW YOU FEEL, BUT YOU HAVE BROKEN THE LAW. CENTURION!

KILL EVERY TENTH MAN IN THIS LEGION.

CAESAR SOON REALISED THAT **DECIMATION WAS TOO SEVERE.** * INSTEAD, HE DECIDED TO KILL EVERY TENTH ONE OF THE **REBEL RINGLEADERS.** WITH THE REBELLION CALMED, HE RETURNED TO ROME...

*DECIMATION WAS KILLING EVERY TENTH PERSON.

...TO FACE A LEGAL PROBLEM...

...BUT YOU CANNOT BE ELECTED CONSUL WITHOUT THE HELP OF THE CURRENT CONSULS WHO...

YES, YES, I KNOW! **WHO** ARE IN MACEDONIA...

THE ONLY WAY FORWARD IS TO BE MADE...

DICTATOR!

AS DICTATOR, CAESAR HAD THE POWER TO MAKE **HIMSELF** A CONSUL FOR 48 BC – AND TO RESTORE THE REPUBLIC.

NOW IT'S TIME TO DEAL WITH POMPEY...

AT POMPEY'S HEADQUARTERS IN MACEDONIA...

WE HAVE PLENTY OF TIME TO PREPARE. EVEN CAESAR WILL NOT ATTEMPT TO CROSS THIS SEA IN THE MIDDLE OF WINTER!.

POMPEY WAS **WRONG.** CAESAR HAD ALREADY SENT SHIPS CARRYING OVER 20,000 MEN. THEY WOULD SET UP A BASE FOR HIM ON MACEDONIAN SOIL. THE BATTLE FOR THE ROMAN REPUBLIC WAS ABOUT TO BEGIN...

CAESAR'S TROOPS SPENT THREE MONTHS WAITING FOR MARK ANTONY TO BRING ACROSS THE REST OF THE ARMY. EVENTUALLY THEY LANDED AT EPIRUS.

CAESAR TOLD HIS GENERALS THE PLAN...

OUR SUPPLIES WON'T LAST LONG. WE MUST TAKE DYRRHACHIUM.

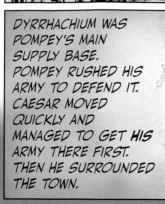

DYRRHACHIUM WAS POMPEY'S MAIN SUPPLY BASE. POMPEY RUSHED HIS ARMY TO DEFEND IT. CAESAR MOVED QUICKLY AND MANAGED TO GET **HIS** ARMY THERE FIRST. THEN HE SURROUNDED THE TOWN.

HIS FORCES WERE STRETCHED VERY THIN. SEVERAL TIMES, POMPEY'S MEN ALMOST BROKE THROUGH. WHEN CAESAR'S ARMY FINALLY ATTACKED, THEY WERE BEATEN BACK.

CAESAR SPOKE TO HIS TROOPS...

DON'T BE SADDENED, MEN. REMEMBER THAT OUR FORTUNES CAN CHANGE...

...MANY OF YOU SERVED WITH ME IN GAUL, WHERE FORTUNE WAS **KIND** TO US...

...NOW, IF WE COME TO HER AID, SHE WILL **SMILE** ON US AGAIN!

CAESAR ORDERED A SERIES OF MARCHES TO DRAW POMPEY'S FORCES AWAY FROM THEIR SUPPLY SHIPS ON THE COAST...

CAESAR'S PLAN WORKED. POMPEY'S ARMY FOLLOWED UNTIL THEY REACHED PHARSALUS.

SCOUTS REPORT THE ENEMY IS CAMPED ACROSS THE PLAIN.

LET'S MOVE OUR CAMP CLOSER TO HIS. I WANT TO BRING HIM OUT.

THREE DAYS LATER...

POMPEY'S MEN ARE MOVING INTO FORMATION.

FINALLY!

HE WILL USE HIS HORSEMEN TO ATTACK OUR RIGHT...

TAKE ONE MAN FROM EACH LEGION OF THE THIRD LINE AND MAKE A FOURTH LINE...

THEN HOLD BACK THE THIRD LINE UNTIL MY SIGNAL. THIS IS VERY IMPORTANT!

ON THE FIELD...

I HAVE ASKED FOR PEACE AT EVERY STAGE AND IT HAS FINALLY COME TO THIS...

IF YOU DIE TODAY, KNOW THAT IT WAS FOR PEACE AND LIBERTY – FOR ROME!

A TRUMPET SOUNDED AND THE FIRST LINE CHARGED...

ROAAAAR!

HALFWAY ACROSS, THEY HALTED...

...AND CHARGED AGAIN.

POMPEY'S HORSEMEN ATTACKED THE RIGHT...

SEND IN THE FOURTH LINE NOW!

FOR HONOUR AND LIBERTY!

THE ASSAULT WAS MORE THAN POMPEY'S FINE HORSEMEN COULD STAND. THEY RETREATED. NOW CAESAR SIGNALLED HIS EXHAUSTED FIRST LINE TO FALL BACK...

...AND REPLACED THEM WITH THE FRESH THIRD LINE...

IT WAS THE LAST STRAW. POMPEY'S ARMY GAVE UP. THEY FLED BACK THROUGH THEIR OWN CAMP...

CAESAR'S MEN FOUND POMPEY'S HEADQUARTERS...

LUCIUS, LOOK AT THIS FEAST!

YES! IT SEEMS THE OLD SENATORS WERE MORE CONCERNED WITH CELEBRATING THE BATTLE THAN ACTUALLY WINNING IT!

LATER...

WELL, WHAT NEWS OF POMPEY?

TO RAISE A FRESH ARMY, NO DOUBT!

THE WORD IS, HE'S GONE TO SEE PTOLEMY.

THEN WE WILL JUST HAVE TO FOLLOW HIM...

...TO EGYPT.

EARLY IN THE CIVIL WAR, PTOLEMY XII HAD HELPED POMPEY. AT 12 YEARS OLD, PTOLEMY RULED EGYPT WITH HIS HALF-SISTER, CLEOPATRA. HOWEVER, THEY WERE ENEMIES.

AS POMPEY NEARED EGYPT...

A BOAT IS COMING TO MEET US.

EXCELLENT! WE WILL BE GREETED WARMLY.

FOUR DAYS LATER, CAESAR ARRIVED IN ALEXANDRIA. HE, TOO, WAS MET BY A WELCOMING PARTY...

...WHO BOARDED CAESAR'S SHIP.

HAIL THE GREAT CAESAR! WE BRING A GIFT IN YOUR HONOUR...

GASP!

THE HEAD OF POMPEY...

POMPEY WAS MY ENEMY, BUT THIS IS NO FIT END FOR A ROMAN! YOU WILL GIVE ME THE REST OF HIM!

ANYWAY, I'M NOT JUST HERE FOR POMPEY.

THIS QUARREL BETWEEN YOUNG PTOLEMY AND HIS SISTER DISTURBS ME...

...AS CONSUL OF ROME, IT IS MY DUTY TO SETTLE THIS DISPUTE.

PTOLEMY HAD DRIVEN CLEOPATRA OUT OF EGYPT.

WHILE CLEOPATRA AND HER ARMY WERE TRAPPED IN PELUSIUM IN JUDEA, CAESAR ENTERED ALEXANDRIA, NOT AS GENERAL BUT AS CONSUL. HE ACTED AS IF EGYPT WAS ALREADY A PROVINCE OF ROME.

THE ALEXANDRIANS ROSE AGAINST CAESAR.

SOME OF HIS SOLDIERS WERE KILLED.

THIS SITUATION IS DANGEROUS. SEND FOR MORE MEN AND SHIPS.

HE SUMMONED A COURT OFFICIAL, THEODOTUS...

TELL PTOLEMY AND HIS SISTER THAT THEY ARE TO STOP THEIR FIGHTING AND COME HERE TO TALK.

A FEW WEEKS LATER...

WHO GOES THERE?

I HAVE A DELIVERY FOR CAESAR FROM QUEEN CLEOPATRA.

IN CAESAR'S QUARTERS...

A GIFT? LEAVE IT IN THE CORNER...

WHAT ARE YOU DOING?

I PRESENT QUEEN CLEOPATRA!

PLOP!

WHIRRRR!

I APOLOGISE FOR THE MANNER OF MY ENTRANCE.

IT WAS UNUSUAL. ALLOW ME TO HELP YOU UP.

I WOULD LIKE THERE TO BE AN ALLIANCE BETWEEN US...

OUR TWO COUNTRIES, THAT IS.

YES, I FEEL THE SAME WAY!

CAESAR OFFERED CLEOPATRA HIS PROTECTION. THEY BECAME VERY CLOSE. THEN PTOLEMY ARRIVED AT THE PALACE WITH HIS ADVISER, POTHINUS.

WHAT'S SHE DOING HERE?

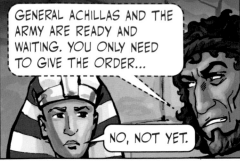

GENERAL ACHILLAS AND THE ARMY ARE READY AND WAITING. YOU ONLY NEED TO GIVE THE ORDER...

NO, NOT YET.

CAESAR TRIED TO CALM THE ANGRY ALEXANDRIANS BY MAKING PEACE BETWEEN PTOLEMY AND CLEOPATRA. HE ALSO HAD LAND THAT HAD BEEN TAKEN FROM ARSINOE, CLEOPATRA'S SISTER, RETURNED TO HER.

BUT THINGS DIDN'T STAY QUIET FOR LONG...

SIR! THE EGYPTIAN ARMY IS ON THE EDGE OF THE CITY!

BANG!

GET THE MEN, SEAL THE PALACE, AND SEND FOR REINFORCEMENTS.

AND PTOLEMY?

ARREST HIM!

DOWNSTAIRS...

THAT OUGHT TO HOLD PTOLEMY'S ARMY FOR A WHILE...

CAESAR, COME QUICKLY!

UP HERE!

IT'S PTOLEMY'S NAVY! WE'RE TRAPPED!

CAESAR ORDERED ALL HIS ARCHERS ONTO THE ROOF...

AIM FOR THE NEAREST SHIPS.

FIRE!

FWIZZZZ!

THE ROMANS SOON CAPTURED THE BOAT.

ONE BY ONE, THEY BOARDED THE REST. THEN THEY SET THE SHIPS ON FIRE...

THEY STORMED THE LIGHTHOUSE...

THE HARBOUR WAS SECURED FOR NOW. CAESAR RETURNED TO THE PALACE.

BAD NEWS! ARSINOE AND GANYMEDES HAVE ESCAPED TO JOIN GENERAL ACHILLAS.*

*GANYMEDES WAS ARSINOE'S MAIN ADVISER.

THIS SITUATION IS GETTING OUT OF HAND!

LATER...

IT IS WELL KNOWN THAT GANYMEDES AND ACHILLAS DON'T GET ALONG. MAYBE...

THEN...

SIR, POTHINUS'S BARBER HAS ASKED TO SEE YOU.

SEND HIM IN.

POTHINUS HAS BEEN SENDING SECRET MESSAGES TO ACHILLAS ON BEHALF OF PTOLEMY!

TREACHERY!

DO YOU HAVE POTHINUS UNDER GUARD?

YES SIR!

KILL HIM.

THE NEXT DAY...

LOOK! GANYMEDES IS HOLDING ACHILLAS'S HEAD UP TO THE CROWD!

SO NOW WE HAVE A NEW ENEMY!

THEY REMAINED TRAPPED.

SIR! GANYMEDES HAS POISONED OUR WELLS!

GET THE MEN TO MAKE NEW ONES – BY TOMORROW!

TWO DAYS LATER, A FRESH LEGION OF SOLDIERS ARRIVED. CAESAR PUT THEM TO WORK, ATTACKING THE NARROW STRIP OF LAND THAT LINKED PHAROS ISLAND TO THE CITY.

EVERYTHING WENT WRONG...

AAAGH! EGYPTIANS! BACK TO THE BOATS!

THERE ARE TOO MANY MEN ON BOARD, SIR. WE CAN'T SET SAIL!

KERRUMPH!

TIME TO GO!

PLOSH!

THERE'S CAESAR IN THE WATER! THROW HIM A LINE!

LOOK, SHE'S SINKING!

AND THE ENEMY HAVE YOUR CLOAK, CAESAR!

CAESAR STAYED TRAPPED IN ALEXANDRIA UNTIL HIS EXTRA TROOPS FINALLY ARRIVED. HE MANAGED TO ESCAPE THE PALACE AND JOIN HIS MEN OUTSIDE THE CITY. IN THE BATTLE THAT FOLLOWED, THE EGYPTIANS WERE QUICKLY DEFEATED AND PTOLEMY WAS KILLED. CAESAR MARCHED INTO ALEXANDRIA AND TOOK A TRIP UP THE NILE RIVER WITH CLEOPATRA.

THIS GREAT LAND COULD NEVER BE A MERE PROVINCE OF ROME.

I WILL LEAVE THREE LEGIONS BEHIND TO SUPPORT YOU...

...AND OUR CHILD.

CAESAR TOOK HIS ARMY TO ASIA MINOR TO FIGHT PHARNACES, SON OF MITHRIDATES. THE BATTLE WAS OVER QUICKLY. CAESAR WAS A PROUD VICTOR...

I CAME, I SAW, I CONQUERED!

IN OCTOBER 47 BC HE RETURNED TO ROME, WHERE HE HAD BEEN ELECTED DICTATOR FOR THE SECOND TIME.

SOON CAME DISTURBING NEWS FROM NORTH AFRICA...

POMPEY'S SONS ARE GATHERING 14 LEGIONS AGAINST US.

ALREADY?

WE ONLY HAVE **SIX** LEGIONS AVAILABLE...

AND **TWO** OF THOSE ARE NEW MEN!

WE WILL JUST HAVE TO GO...

THAPSUS, NORTH AFRICA - EARLY 46 BC.

CAESAR, WE ARE READY!

LET US GO!

YOU WILL WAIT FOR MY ORDER!

SUDDENLY, A TRUMPET SOUNDED.

WHAT THE — ?

CHARGE!

GOOD LUCK!

CHAAARGE!

AGAIN, THE BATTLE WAS SOON OVER.

WANG!

WURRRAAAGH!

CAESAR SPENT THE NEXT THREE MONTHS IN THE ROMAN PROVINCES IN AFRICA THAT HE HAD SEIZED FROM POMPEY'S ALLY, KING JUBA. HIS OLD ENEMY, CATO, KILLED HIMSELF.

EVEN THOUGH POMPEY'S SONS ESCAPED, THE CIVIL WAR WAS OVER FOR NOW.

IN OCTOBER 46 BC, MAGNIFICENT CELEBRATIONS WERE HELD FOR CAESAR. THE LONG PARADE MARCHED DOWN STREETS LINED WITH TREASURES AND PICTURES OF THE BATTLES.

IN EACH TRIUMPH THERE WAS A DISPLAY OF PRISONERS...

VERCINGETORIX, WHO WAS KILLED AFTER THE PARADE...

KING JUBA'S SON, WHO LATER BECAME A KING HIMSELF...

CAESAR RODE IN A CHARIOT PULLED BY THREE WHITE HORSES. AFTERWARDS, THERE WERE DAYS OF SHOWS, GAMES, FIGHTS, AND FEASTING AT 22,000 TABLES.

AND CLEOPATRA'S SISTER, ARSINOE. THE CROWDS ALL CHEERED HER.

CAESAR MADE SURE HE WAS REMEMBERED IN STONE. BUILDINGS LIKE THE NEW FORUM JULIUM IN THE CENTRE OF ROME WERE BUILT IN HIS HONOUR.

THE HIGHLIGHT WAS THE TEMPLE OF GENETRIX – THE HOME OF A VERY SPECIAL STATUE.

WHAT DO YOU THINK OF IT?

IT'S BEAUTIFUL – I'M HONOURED.

CLEOPATRA HAD COME TO VISIT WITH HER YOUNG SON, CAESARION.

BUT I'M ALSO PUZZLED. WHERE IS YOUR STATUE?

YOUR CONQUESTS RIVAL THOSE OF ALEXANDER THE GREAT. AS HE WAS, SO SHOULD YOU BE – A GOD TO YOUR PEOPLE!

DECEMBER 46 BC.

13 LEGIONS AND 3,000 HORSES?

AND THEY'RE MASSING ON THE SPANISH BORDER, SIR...

POMPEY'S SONS HAD RENEWED THE FIGHT.

WILL THIS WAR EVER BE OVER?

MUNDA, SOUTHERN SPAIN – MARCH 45 BC.

CAESAR! THE TENTH LEGION IS FOLDING!

AAAGH!

WRAAAGH!

CAESAR'S LEGION OF VETERAN SOLDIERS SEEMED TO BE GIVING UP.

GNNNGH!

SLICE!

CAESAR'S MEN BEGAN TO FLEE.

YOU! GET BACK IN THE LINE AND ORDER THE OTHERS TO DO THE SAME!

STANDARD BEARERS – HOLD YOUR GROUND!

BY A GREAT EFFORT, THE FINAL BATTLE OF THE CIVIL WAR WAS WON. OVER 30,000 OF THE ENEMY WERE KILLED. AT THE END, A TIRED CAESAR SPOKE...

I HAVE FOUGHT FOR VICTORY OFTEN ENOUGH, BUT THIS IS THE FIRST TIME...

...I HAVE HAD TO FIGHT FOR MY LIFE!

AT LAST, CAESAR COULD TURN HIS ATTENTION TO ROME AND THE PROBLEMS THERE. HE AGREED TO CARRY ON AS DICTATOR FOR ANOTHER TEN YEARS.

CAESAR INCREASED THE SIZE OF THE SENATE. HALF OF THE NEW MEMBERS CAME FROM OUTSIDE ROME. THIS HELPED HIS GREAT LAND LAW. THERE WERE TO BE 40 NEW COMMUNITIES IN THE PROVINCES FOR BOTH WAR VETERANS AND THE 80,000 ROMANS FROM THE CAPITAL.

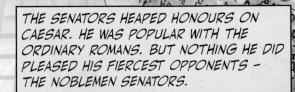

THE SENATORS HEAPED HONOURS ON CAESAR. HE WAS POPULAR WITH THE ORDINARY ROMANS. BUT NOTHING HE DID PLEASED HIS FIERCEST OPPONENTS – THE NOBLEMEN SENATORS.

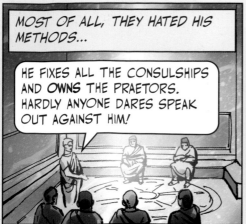

MOST OF ALL, THEY HATED HIS METHODS...

HE FIXES ALL THE CONSULSHIPS AND **OWNS** THE PRAETORS. HARDLY ANYONE DARES SPEAK OUT AGAINST HIM!

AND THOSE THAT DO JUST ROUSE HIS **ANGER!**

CAESAR RUNS THIS COUNTRY LIKE A GENERAL. IT IS AS IF HE WERE A **KING!**

MEANWHILE, CAESAR WAS BUSY PLANNING...

MARK ANTONY, I STILL HAVE ONE WAR LEFT TO FIGHT...

IT HAS TO BE AGAINST THE PARTHIANS! IF ANYONE CAN CONQUER THEM, YOU CAN, CAESAR!

BUT I NEED TO MAKE SURE MY CHANGES ARE CARRIED THROUGH WHILE I AM AWAY.

ACTING AS CONSUL, CAESAR MADE HIMSELF DICTATOR FOR LIFE. THE DATE OF 18TH MARCH, 44 BC – THE IDES OF MARCH – WAS SET FOR HIS DEPARTURE TO FIGHT THE PARTHIANS. TWO KNIGHTS, OPPIUS AND BALBUS, WOULD BE LEFT IN CHARGE OF THE SENATE. THIS OUTRAGED A GROUP OF SENATORS, WHO BEGAN MEETING IN SECRET.

SENATOR LONGINUS LED THE MEETING...

SO THIS IS IT! WE ARE TO BE GOVERNED BY CAESAR'S KNIGHTS?!

THEN LONGINUS'S BROTHER-IN-LAW, MARCUS BRUTUS, SPOKE...

IT IS AS CICERO SAID: ALL THE PRECIOUS THINGS WORTH HAVING – COUNTRY, HONOUR, RESPECT – HAVE **GONE!**

WE MUST ACT AS ONE. CAESAR MUST BE STOPPED!

AFTER CAESAR

Roman democracy had been in disorder for nearly 50 years. The assassination of Caesar marked the end of the republic. Afterwards, Rome was ruled by emperors.

AFTERMATH OF THE ASSASSINATION

Before Caesar's funeral, many Romans were on the side of Brutus and his fellow assassins. Public opinion was quickly changed when Caesar's dead body was put on display and his co-consul, Mark Antony, gave a funeral speech. Caesar had named Octavian, his adopted son, as his successor. Antony and Octavian each took half of the empire. Eventually, they fought one another for power. Octavian won and became the first Roman emperor. Before long, it was said that every one of Caesar's assassins was dead. Some committed suicide, while others were murdered.

Brutus led the conspiracy against Caesar. He committed suicide in 42 BC after being defeated by Antony and Octavian.

CLEOPATRA'S DOWNFALL

After Caesar's assassination, Cleopatra went back to Egypt with their son, Caesarion. Antony, who now held power in the east, allowed her to rule Egypt and Cyprus. She became his ally and, though he was married to Octavian's sister, they fell in love. Cleopatra and Antony had three children together. Antony gave each child a part of the Roman empire. In 31 BC, Octavian fought Antony in a famous naval battle at Actium and won. Antony committed suicide by stabbing himself. Cleopatra also committed suicide by allowing a poisonous snake to bite her.

In this Egyptian relief of Cleopatra, she is dressed as the goddess Isis.

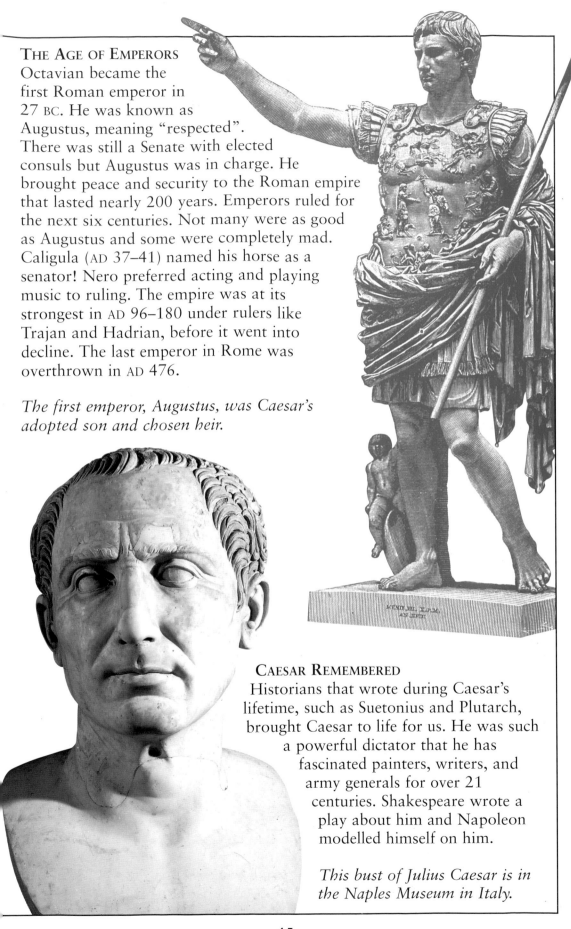

THE AGE OF EMPERORS

Octavian became the first Roman emperor in 27 BC. He was known as Augustus, meaning "respected". There was still a Senate with elected consuls but Augustus was in charge. He brought peace and security to the Roman empire that lasted nearly 200 years. Emperors ruled for the next six centuries. Not many were as good as Augustus and some were completely mad. Caligula (AD 37–41) named his horse as a senator! Nero preferred acting and playing music to ruling. The empire was at its strongest in AD 96–180 under rulers like Trajan and Hadrian, before it went into decline. The last emperor in Rome was overthrown in AD 476.

The first emperor, Augustus, was Caesar's adopted son and chosen heir.

CAESAR REMEMBERED

Historians that wrote during Caesar's lifetime, such as Suetonius and Plutarch, brought Caesar to life for us. He was such a powerful dictator that he has fascinated painters, writers, and army generals for over 21 centuries. Shakespeare wrote a play about him and Napoleon modelled himself on him.

This bust of Julius Caesar is in the Naples Museum in Italy.

GLOSSARY

alliance An agreement to work together.

assassination The murder of someone who is well known or important.

conspiracy A secret plan or plot made by two or more people.

crucify To put someone to death by tying or nailing to a cross.

debts Amounts of money or something else that you owe.

descended Belonging to a later generation of the same family.

dictator In early Roman times, a consul who was given complete power in a crisis. Later it meant someone who has complete control of a country.

Etruscans People who lived in Etruria, now part of modern-day Italy.

legion A unit of the Roman army containing approximately 5,000 men.

patrician A member of one of the noble families of ancient Rome.

plebeian Of or relating to the common people of ancient Rome.

province An outlying area of a country, away from the centre of population.

ransom Money that is demanded before someone who is being held captive can be set free.

rebellion When people rise up against their leader or ruler.

republic A country or state in which the people elect representatives who manage the government.

sacred Holy.

scheming To plan or plot something, especially in secret or dishonestly.

spoils Valuable things taken from the defeated by the winners after a war.

suicide To kill oneself.

treachery Being disloyal.

treason The crime of betraying your country.

tribune In ancient Rome, the elected officer who spoke in the Senate on behalf of the plebeians.

triumvirate A group of three people responsible for a specific job.

FOR MORE INFORMATION

ORGANISATIONS

The British Museum
Great Russell Street
London
WC1B 3DG
Website:
www.thebritishmuseum.ac.uk

Ashmolean Museum of Art and
Archaeology
Beaumont Street
Oxford
OX1 2PH
www.ashmol.ox.ac.uk

Roman Legionary Museum
High Street
Caerleon
NP18 1AE
Wales

Roman Baths
Pump Room
Stall Street
Bath
BA1 1LZ
www.romanbaths.co.uk

Fishbourne Roman Palace
Salthill Road
Fishbourne
Chichester
PO19 2QR

Canterbury Roman Museum
Butchery Lane
Canterbury
www.canterbury-museum.co.uk

FOR FURTHER READING
If you liked this book, you might also want to try:

How to be a Roman Soldier
by Fiona Macdonald, Book House 2005

Battle Zones: Warfare in the Ancient World
by Mark Bergin, Book House 2003

You Wouldn't Want to be a Roman Gladiator!
by John Malam, Hodder Wayland 2002

Spectacular Visual Guides: A Roman Fort
by Stephen Johnson, Book House 2005

INDEX

Websites

Due to the changing nature of internet links, the Salariya Book Company has developed an online list of websites related to the subject of this book. This site is updated regularly. Please use this link to access the list:

http://www.book-house.co.uk/gnf/caesar